Empath

A guide to understanding your infinite intelligence. The ancient knowledge within you.

Frank Knoll

Disclaimer:

© 2019 – TWK - Publishing. All Rights Reserved.

No part of this publication may be reproduced, stored or transmitted in any form or by any means – electronic, mechanical, scanning, photocopying, recording or otherwise, without prior written permission from the author.

This publication is provided for informational and educational purposes only and cannot be used as a substitute for expert medical advice. The information contained herein does not take into account an individual reader's health or medical history.

Hence, it's important to consult with a health care professional before starting any regimen mentioned herein. Though all possible efforts have been made in the preparation of this eBook, the author makes no warranties as to the accuracy or completeness of its contents.

The readers understand that they can follow the information, guidelines and ideas mentioned in this eBook at their own risk. All trademarks mentioned are the property of their respective owners.

Table of Contents

Chapter 1 - What is an Empath?..1

Chapter 2 - Different Types of Empath........................5

Chapter 3 - Famous Empaths in History 13

Chapter 4 - How to Tell If You're an Empath 23

Chapter 5 - Is Empathy A Sign of Intelligence?........30

Chapter 6 - How to Harness Your Empath Gift.........37

Chapter 7 - Is Being an Empath a Superpower or a Super-Stressor? 44

Chapter 8 - The Benefits of Being an Empath 49

Chapter 9 - Ancient Knowledge and Infinite Intelligence...58

Chapter 10 - Why You Must Be Careful.......................65

Chapter 1
What is an Empath?

Empaths are highly-sensitive individuals who have the uncanny ability to read other people and be in tune with their feelings or what they are going through. They experience an intense level of compassion and understanding that they absorb deep emotions that only hypersensitive people could recognize. They experience a powerful sense of empathy and concern beyond normal tendencies. It is akin to being able to read true emotions by breaking through the façade that other people put up to hide their feelings. More often than not, true empaths can sense emotions that are deeper than what is being projected on the surface.

Not all empaths understand that they have the gift of empathy. Some of them may not be aware that the experience happens involuntarily. It is in their nature to act compassionately, and they don't need to trigger something to unleash such ability. They could experience empathy toward friends, family, or strangers throughout their lives.

Some empaths are also more in tune with nature, environment, or animals. This is why there are people who seem to communicate well with animals and know how to handle them when others had given up on them.

There are also empaths who feel a strong connection to the heavenly bodies or planetary system, so when there are shifts and movements in the cosmos, they sense the energies and understand the message that these movements bring. Some empaths are so gifted that they not only can interpret the anomalies from a distance, but they also can affect or influence these energies. This is similar to how true empaths can make sense of the emotional blocks and burden that people carry with them. They seem to know how to create an opportunity to help.

All empaths are highly sensitive, but not all highly sensitive people are empaths. Generally, people can empathize with others when a situation calls for it, such as a change in life circumstances, or a tragedy. Being an empath is more than just being emphatic to someone who is in dire straits.

Although empaths share similar traits with highly sensitive people, empaths take the experience further by sensing subtle energies and absorbing them. This means that if a person or an environment is giving off energies, empaths absorb them into their bodies, so they experience emotions and physical sensations in ways that no other highly sensitive people can.

The ability to absorb other people's energies allows an empath to internalize the emotions and feelings of others. So, all the unwanted feelings of pain, discomfort, suffering, grief, or sorrow are somehow absorbed by the empath. This is on top of what the empaths are feeling based on their experiences. When all the feelings converge, it is possible that empaths may have trouble distinguishing other people's feelings from their own. So, the experience can be burdensome, thereby taking a toll on them physically and emotionally.

Whether being an empath is a gift or a curse, remains to be a topic of debate. It could be a curse if it becomes too emotionally draining, or it can be a gift if it is harnessed properly and put into good use. The first step is to recognize the ability and acknowledge its presence. An enlightened empath would know what to do with his gifts to experience a full and purposeful life.

Chapter 2
Different Types of Empath

Being an empath and a highly sensitive individual are not mutually exclusive. A person can be both within the emphatic spectrum—with varying intensities and inclinations. In general, empaths are perceptive and sensitive to what other people are giving off. It could be energy, feelings, emotions, or messages. However, empaths can be categorized into six main types based on their receptiveness to certain situations and how they react to their surroundings.

1. **Emotional**

    Emotional empaths can easily pick up the emotions of people they interact with or those around them. They do not only absorb the deep emotions, but they also experience the intense feelings as if they were their very own. When the emotions are negative, like pain, sadness, or grief, they could be extremely draining to the empaths because they not only have to deal with their own emotions, but they also have to consider the emotions of others.

There are situations wherein emotional empaths could have a difficult time separating their emotions from those of others. With a proper understanding of the gift they possess, emotional empaths can develop the ability to recognize other people's emotions and use that ability to heal others emotionally.

2. Physical

Physical or Medical empaths are people who intuitively know when a person is sick or is dealing with health issues. They can pick up on the energy released by the body in the form of physical symptoms that they feel in their own body.

In some cases, physical empaths can detect blockages in the person's energy flow, which can manifest in diseases if the blockages are not cleared. Physical empaths can have the ability to clear energy blocks if they have some form of training in the realm of alternative healing.

Physical empaths have a keen awareness of how their body reacts when interacting with someone who is ill. In extreme cases, they exhibit the same physical symptoms and feel that they have acquired the diseases as well. Absorbing the symptoms can lead to potential health problems in the future if the physical empaths do not learn to let go of the negative energy that they had picked up from other people. Without defenses and boundaries, physical empaths can end up with empathic illnesses that manifest in the form of anxiety, depression, panic disorders, pain, or mysterious ailments that come and go.

There are ways to stop absorbing other people's pain and illness, and they involve setting limits and boundaries when interacting with people that are energy vampires. Learning to surrender and letting go of the toxic energy can help physical empaths to evolve and use their abilities to help others heal.

3. Plant

Plant empaths are people who are highly attuned to the needs of plants and trees. They possess the unique ability to recognize and identify the right plant for the right garden, home, or patch of land. They are likely to choose an occupation where they can work in gardens, parks, orchards, or wild landscapes where there are trees, plants, and greeneries. People with this gift have an exceptional connection to plants and trees, and it goes deeper than just being adept at growing plants and taking care of them.

Plant empaths can sense the energy given off by plants and trees and interpret the message as guidance on how to be more in tune with their needs. People who recognize early on that are plant empaths, acknowledge the need to be surrounded by trees and plants. They make a lot of contact with them to absorb their energy and receive physical and emotional signals and messages.

4. Geomantic

Geomantic empaths can read and interpret the energy and signals transmitted by the earth through the physical environment and landscape. They are extremely in tune to the natural world, and they grieve when damage is done in the environment. It is natural for geomantic empaths to feel a deep connection to certain places or locations with historical significance. They are instinctively drawn to places that hold sacred power such us churches, groves, temples, and sacred mountains.

Being a geomantic empath means being very sensitive to the history of a place that it is not uncommon to pick up on sadness, grief, or fear from locations with a storied past, especially those that were ravaged by war. On the flip side, geomantic empaths can also pick up on joy, happiness, and other positive feelings in places where good things have occurred.

Empaths who have a deep connection with nature would find that helping in projects that help the environment and can be a form of healing. This means that a beautiful and harmonious environment make geomantic empaths feel happier, centered, and balanced. Being one with nature allows empaths to recharge and shake off any negative emotions they had absorbed from their interactions.

5. Animal

Animal empaths have a deep and strong connection to animals, and they are likely to devote their time working to ensure the welfare of animals. Those who possess this gift can telepathically communicate with animals and creatures that's why they have a deeper understanding of the needs of the animals.

Empaths who fall under this type are likely to spend as much time with animals as they possibly could because it is in their nature to nurture animals of various shapes and sizes.

The constant interaction allows them to determine what is wrong with the animals skillfully and they can heal them. Many animal empaths hone their skills by studying the biology and psychology of animals. The more they train, the better they become at healing animals.

6. Intuitive

Intuitive empaths, also known as claircognizant empaths, and can get an insight from other people simply by being around them. Those with a keen sense of intuition don't even need to interact with people to pick up information physically. With just a flitting look, intuitive empaths can sense if someone is lying or telling the truth.

They can gauge if a person has good or bad intentions.

It is believed that intuitive empaths have telepathic abilities that allow them to penetrate through other people's energy fields. It is akin to having telepathic abilities where empaths can read other people's thoughts. The more aligned an intuitive empath is to a person, the more accurate the readings would be.

Having the ability to read minds or energies is an incredibly powerful gift that can only get better with training. The downside with having this gift is that there is a tendency to be bombarded with thoughts and emotions of other people that they become too overwhelming and difficult to manage. Those who possess this ability are advised to strengthen their energetic field so that they have control of the energy and the information that they absorb. Otherwise, it can be taxing to the mind and the body.

Chapter 3
Famous Empaths in History

Mahatma Gandhi

Mahatma Gandhi was a great master of empathy. Gandhi had already been fighting for the rights of Indians in South Africa for more than two decades when he decided it was time to return to his country in 1915 to help campaign for Indian independence. To understand the struggles of his countrymen, he ditched his fancy barrister clothes, wrapped himself in a loincloth, and stepped into the shoes of peasant farmers. He needed to experience the day-to-day life of the poorest of the poor in India.

Gandhi's deep empathetic instinct connected him to the people, and he absorbed the pain and suffering caused by the British rule. He did not merely observe the plight of his people; he lived through the hardships and witnessed the abuse and the cruelty firsthand.

Because of his deep sense of empathy towards his countrymen, he was able to campaign for independence effectively. His words and actions resonated with the people because he was authentic and he was genuinely concerned about the plight of his people.

Gandhi walked the path of the impoverished and the underprivileged, stripping himself of his ascetic lifestyle in a bold attempt to understand the suffering of the Indian people. His gift of empathy made him more sensitive to any situation, and he intuitively knew what to do to move a crowd or calm them down. Even in the face of violent strife, Gandhi remained unfazed because he used his hypersensitivity to appeal to people's sense of decency and humanity to maintain peace and cooperation despite the differences in beliefs.

Mother Theresa

Mother Theresa is the epitome of empathy. Her compassion and kindness helped a lot of people in need, especially the poorest of the poor. She had the innate ability to make people feel they mattered. Her presence gave people hope and courage to endure hardships. She founded the Missionaries of the Charity Sisters, which ministers to the poor in the slums of Calcutta, India.

Through her missionary works, Mother Theresa tended to the sick, fed the starving, and comforted the dying. She showed that despite the seemingly unending suffering and adversities in life, humanity and compassion could make a huge difference. The enormity of her calling could be perceived as a huge burden, knowing fully well the impossibility of her aspiration. But her compassion and kindness gave people hope and restored faith in humanity. The sick had access to healing, and the dying were treated with dignity and compassion in their final hours.

Mother Theresa's corporal works of mercy espoused the views and teachings of the Catholic Church, but her ministry helped the poor and the sick regardless of their religious affiliations. Her actions were motivated by compassion and love for the impoverished people. Her motivation was purely altruistic.

As an empath, Mother Theresa was drawn toward people who are in physical pain, in emotional distress, or in dire situations that needed resolution. She understood and gave them the validation and support that they needed. The need to help them stemmed from having the capacity to feel and share the emotions of those who suffer.

Princess Diana

One of the most recognizable personalities in the world is the late Princess Diana. Even before she married into the royal family and became a princess, she had already shown signs that she was an empath. She had worked in childcare which signified that she had compassion for children and advocated for their well-being.

It is when she became a princess that her gift of empathy shone brighter. She had the amazing ability to connect with people on an intimately personal, level as well as, in huge crowds. She had engaged in numerous charitable works even after her divorce from Prince Charles.

Even though her life had been very public, and she struggled to shut down her sensitivity to other people, she used it as an opportunity to shine the spotlight away from her celebrity and focused it on her projects that she was passionate about.

Millions of people around the world were drawn to her not just because of her charm and beauty, but because of her empathetic abilities and compassion for the people in need. She was able to advocate against land mines and fought to bring awareness about AIDS when people living with the disease were being shunned from society.

St. Francis of Assisi

Before he became St. Francis of Assisi, Giovanni di Pietro di Bernardone was a son of a wealthy merchant who went on a pilgrimage in Rome at the age of 23. He was struck by the blatant contrast between the opulence within St. Peter's Basilica and the poverty that surrounded it as beggars asked for alms from churchgoers. In a show of empathy, Bernadone persuaded one of the beggars to exchange clothes with him and spent the day in tattered clothes begging for alms.

It was a turning point in Bernadone's life which led to him founding a religious order whose brothers worked to help the poor and the sick. They gave up their wealth and worldly possession to live in poverty. Perhaps the ultimate show of compassion and kindness is when he hugged the lepers whose bodies were mangled and withered by the disease. At that time, lepers were treated less than humans by the society because of how they looked. People avoided them like the plague for fear that they might catch the dreaded disease.

Only someone with an emphatic ability can do what St. Francis of Assisi did. His love, dedication, and loyalty to God manifested in his gifts which he extended to the poor, the sick, and the needy. He lived in abject poverty to understand and share in the suffering and pain of the people he helped. Through his actions, St. Francis of Assisi made full use of his God-given gift of empathy and created the largest religious movement whose mission is to serve the poor and the disadvantaged.

Nelson Mandela

After the death of his father, Nelson Mandela was sent to live with the leader of the Thembu tribe where his father was a counselor to the acting king. He was groomed for leadership and was exposed to the ways of the council, having sat at council meetings to observe and gain an understanding of tribal leadership. He was sent to the best schools and lived a life of privilege. He ran away from the tribe to avoid an arranged marriage.

It was in 1941 when Mandela was faced with the brutal reality of apartheid. The racial divide in South Africa has made the country a ticking time bomb. He experienced first-hand what black life was like in urban South Africa. It was the turning point in his life, and he knew he had to do something about the injustice and oppression.

Mandela joined an underground movement to help fight racial segregation and put an end to white supremacy. His advocacy was motivated by his genuine compassion for the black South Africans who were treated unjustly and attacked viciously. He not only understood the pain and suffering of his countrymen, but he also felt them. He was a man of deep empathy, and he used this gift to persuade both friends and enemies that the civil unrest could have a peaceful end.

He was marked as a threat to the racist government, so in 1962, he was imprisoned for conspiring to overthrow the state. During his incarceration, resistance to apartheid took different forms throughout the tumultuous years of civil unrest. Non-violent demonstrations shifted to impassioned protests, to strikes, to political actions, and eventually, to armed resistance.

Mandela was made to look like a terrorist, but the reality was that he believed that common humanity and decency still exist in the hearts of his enemies. With his empathic abilities, he was able to prevent a catastrophic civil war that could have destroyed South Africa. Even after his death, his life's work continues to rectify the damages caused by the apartheid regime.

Jane Goodall

Jane Goodall is a world-renowned primatologist who had made historic breakthroughs and discoveries about chimpanzees and their behavior. Although her research and life's work are mainly on primates, she also advocated for the protection of habitats and the well-being of wild and captive animals. She spent most of her time traveling around the world to raise awareness about animal welfare and forest protection.

In her talks and speeches, she emphasized the role of empathy in taking care of animals and the importance of the interaction of children with pets. She believes that if young children grow up with animals, they could learn and understand empathy towards animals. She considers empathy as a way to bring humans closer to reaching their highest potential.

Goodall's empathetic ability focuses on the capacity to understand and communicate with animals and other living creatures on earth. She is particularly knowledgeable about chimpanzees, and she can read their intentions and behaviors. It is possible that with her constant interaction with chimpanzees, there is some level of transference of emotions which allows her to interpret the natural tones and noises that the animals convey.

Primal empaths have a heightened sensitivity towards animals and can get through the communication barrier between humans and animals. This is why Goodall can form a profound relationship with chimpanzees she rehabilitated and sent back into the wild. In the same vein, Goodall can also feel the suffering and pain of the animals who have been abused by humans. Her empathy towards animals motivated her to raise awareness about endangered species, global warming, deforestation, animal abuse, and other hard issues that affect animals and the environment.

Chapter 4
How to Tell If You're an Empath

Being an empath means having the innate ability to feel another's person's positive and negative emotions. It is different from just being empathetic to someone because something tragic had happened. Empaths always have trouble separating their feelings from that of other people's feelings.

Empaths are hardwired to feel that way because they absorb other people's positive and negative energies into their bodies. Unlike sympathetic people, true empaths soak up energies even when there are no obvious inciting incidents like a death in the family, a divorce, or a trauma. Empaths don't choose what feelings to absorb; they simply sense whatever is being given off.

According to science, empaths have a hyperactive mirror neuron system in the brain. This means that they have a specialized group of cells in the brain that are responsible for compassion, empathy, and kindness are thought to be extremely heightened. As a result, receptors are overly sensitive that they can absorb energies from other people or even objects.

The experience can be overwhelming, and it can be difficult for the empaths to separate what they are truly feeling from that of the other person. Having a greater intuition and compassion can create a deeper connection with people, whether friends or strangers. However, living in a constant state high sensitivity comes with its challenges and disadvantages.

If empaths are not aware that they hold this special ability, they will find themselves over-stimulated, overwhelmed, and exhausted each time they absorb all the stress and negativity from the people they come in contact with it.

To empaths, everyday interactions may be difficult to tolerate. All the different feelings and emotions that they absorb could cause them stress and anxiety, especially when they could not separate other people's emotions from their own. Heightened sensitivity can take its toll on the physical, mental, and emotional well-being of empaths. Those who are not able to tolerate the assault to the senses are inclined to turn to food, alcohol, and drugs to handle the empathy overload.

Taking charge of the sensitivities is important to harness the spell gift of empathy so that the empaths can enrich not only their lives but the lives of others too. However, certain empaths must be able to determine if they are, indeed, true empaths. It starts by identifying their special empath talents and evaluating if they are innate or event-triggered. To determine if they are empaths and distinguish themselves from sympathetic people, they can do a self-assessment test.

The self-assessment test entails answering a set of questions that determine how strong the emphatic tendencies of a person is. There are variations to self-assessment questions that are floating around, and they pretty much have the same ideas. The questionnaire is very straightforward, and they're answerable by a "Yes" or a "No." Answering "Yes" to most questions would ascertain if a person is an empath and would determine the level of their emphatic propensities.

Answering the questions can quickly determine the level and intensity of a person's tendencies along the empathic spectrum, but it is also important—perhaps even more important—to understand what the questions signify.

Alternatively, one can look at the telltale signs that empaths share across the spectrum. These signs not only help in assessing if they are empaths, but it also helps them understand their abilities better. These signs separate true empaths from people who are just sensitive.

Empaths do not have filters

Empaths carry the distinction of not having filters like regular people do. They absorb what is going on around them like human sponges. They are not able to filter out the things that come to them. It can be noise, smell, energy, or emotions. They do not have the chance to block them out as they come nor have the opportunity to refuse the sensations. They are not able to select only the positive or pleasurable ones—they take everything in. Their gifts of intuition and compassion are not selective. So, whatever comes to them, in whatever shape or sensation, are felt by empaths.

This is the main reason why the self-assessment questionnaire asks about being easily overwhelmed or exhausted in social situations even after short periods of interaction. Empaths almost always feel tired because they don't have an inner system to filter all the energies that bombard their senses.

Empaths need to recharge alone

People with heightened sensitivities need to recharge, and they need to do it alone. This means sleeping and unwinding by themselves. Alone time may be difficult for other people to comprehend, especially if they are in happy and fulfilling relationships, but it is necessary for empaths as a way to catch their breath, clear their minds, release negative energies and recover their mental and physical strength to face another day. Partners of empaths should be cognizant of this need so that it does not fracture their relationships or create tensions at home.

Empaths have trouble setting boundaries

Since empaths have a keen sense of compassion and kindness towards others, it is difficult for them to set boundaries. This is because they feel like they are disappointing people whenever they say no or turn their backs on something that they couldn't handle. When they say no, they feel like they are letting people down and this weighs heavily on them and adds to their emotional load.

Another possible problem that this could bring is an opportunity for people to take advantage of the situation. Unable to refuse requests or favors, empaths are targets for abuse especially by people who show flashes of narcissism. Without setting boundaries, empaths could find themselves being manipulated by other people and have no way to get out of the situation unless there is an intervention.

Empaths know that they have a special gift, but most of the time they do not understand their situation. The self-assessment questionnaire and the signs can give them a better understanding of the empath skills they possess. It will also make them realize that it is not something to be scared of. Instead, it is something to be celebrated because it is a gift that can help other people in immeasurable ways.

Chapter 5
Is Empathy A Sign of Intelligence?

Empathy is an innate ability that can be too complex to understand without a clear context. It is established that highly sensitive people who have a high level of empathy and compassion towards others. Everyone has a natural tendency to empathize with others because humans are simply built that way. However, not all humans have the empathetic ability to feel and discern what other people are feeling just by looking at them. It begs the question: Is empathy a sign of higher intelligence?

One can argue that intelligence does not play that big role because empaths operate on feelings, emotions, and to a certain extent, and psychic abilities. This is an understandable argument, but it is highly flawed and inconsistent with scientific explanations of intelligence.

Others argue that intelligence and emotions are interrelated, in that, one cannot separate the two. Going by that argument, intelligence plays a role in empathy and vice versa, which signifies that empaths are not only emotionally sensitive but highly intelligent as well. This is a more sound argument because several theories had put forward that intelligence and cognition are important aspects of emotion.

Empaths act primarily on the emotions that they absorb from other people, but there are still essential mental processes involved in recognizing events, assessing situations, and interpreting messages. To answer the question put forward, it is necessary to understand the connection between empathy and intelligence. The role they play in social interaction can explain their symbiotic relationship. It is the link that can help understand empathetic abilities and sensitivities.

Role of Empathy on Intelligence

Empathy is correlated with a type of intelligence called emotional intelligence or commonly known as EQ (emotional quotient). In the cognitive sense of being tremendously skilled at understanding other people's feelings and their behaviors, empathy is a sign of intelligence. However, it would be too limiting to think of it this way because empathy is a multi-dimensional ability. It has the cognitive dimension, as well as, the emotional and behavioral dimensions.

Regarding compassion and caring, empathy is more influenced by morals and values more than intelligence. These two, in turn, are affected by upbringing, environment, and to a certain extent, religion. However, the decision on how to act requires a certain level of intelligence and cognitive skills. Furthermore, empaths require strong cognitive skills to perform various mental activities. Without such skills, it would be difficult for empaths to function and bring balance to their lives.

A person's sense of empathy can be tested in social interactions. It is through social behavior that one's level of responsiveness to the needs of other people can be assessed. It has been established that true empathy is something that's innate and people born with it have a greater sensitivity to what other people are trying to convey.

Through empathy, there is recognition of other people's emotions. Although it is intuitive, it does not mean that the process ends there. To make sense of the messages that are being conveyed, empaths have to process them so that they make decisions on how to act. Such decision-making requires a level of intelligence for the process to be executed properly.

Take the case of a person who shares a tragic experience to a highly sensitive individual. The limbic brain of the empath processes the information and quickly searches from memory for a similar experience where the same feelings had registered. When the memory comes back, the empath identifies with the grieving person and commiserates with him or her.

Thus, intelligence plays a role in how empaths internalize the emotions of other people.

Intelligence, whether cognitive or emotional, guides empaths on how to act, and react when they absorb negative energies and emotions. It directs them to act in the most appropriate manner possible with the intention of helping the distressed individual.

In a study that analyzed the link between empathy and emotional intelligence, it was found out that cognitive dimensions and emotional clarity influence the nurses' attitudes and potential behavior in a patient care setting. What this means is that nurses who have empathic abilities and high emotional intelligence tend to have desirable attitudes and behaviors that can improve the quality of care in patients. They can provide compassionate care to patients, which adds to the level of satisfaction of patients. This, in turn, creates a deeper and more meaningful nurse-patient relationship.

Connecting emotionally to someone who is going through a difficult time is intuitive for empaths. But to understand, process, and interpret their emotions, it requires not just sensitivity and insight, but also intelligence as well. Empathy, thus, is a cornerstone of professions devoted to helping others, which includes medical practitioners, caregivers, nurses, social workers, counselors, community volunteers, and wildlife carers, to name just a few.

The brain is hard-wired for empathy because it provides a language to interpret the feelings and emotions of other people. The interpretation links up to the empath's physical reaction and the corresponding action. Without emotional and cognitive intelligence, empaths will most likely have a difficulty comprehending the situation, more so in interpreting the message being conveyed.

The same idea applies to non-verbal cues like facial expression, the tone of voice, and posture. Empaths can also detect subtle changes in body language or intonation of voice, and can accurately read these cues. This is because empaths, with their acute sensitivities, intuitively pay more attention to details. They read more into the nonverbal cues because the real message sometimes cannot be expressed in words alone.

Being an empath is not just about emotions and feelings; it is a complex combination of cognitive skills, emotional intelligence, and moral compass. It is a multifaceted ability that directly impacts the many areas of life, including relationships, social interactions, career and work life, and spiritual inclinations. It requires a high level of intelligence and soundness of mind to keep these aspects in balance. Empathy and intelligence are deeply intertwined that it would be impossible for an empath to lead a balanced life without intellectual aptitude to handle all the things they absorb from other people. As such, it is safe to say that empathy is a sign of intelligence.

Chapter 6
How to Harness Your Empath Gift

Empathy can happen voluntarily or involuntary. For true empaths, it is largely involuntary and something that cannot be fully controlled when it happens. Interactions can lead to information overload and energy drain. This is when empaths feel the weight of their gifts and start to wonder if all their special abilities are worth having.

The sad truth is that many people who are capable of empathy have trouble adjusting to their empath gifts once they recognize they have them. What's worse is that they have no clue how to start harnessing them, and they go about it the wrong way. Instead of being positive about it, they develop negative mindsets that lead to mental disorders. People in the empathetic community are constantly haunted by the fear of not being able to control the gifts they have. As a result, they are always doubting themselves and keeping themselves too guarded.

Empaths are always dealing with mental, physical, and spiritual strain because they overexert themselves when compassion level goes on overdrive. They must understand that it could not go on for long periods without proper training and guidance. The goal is to harness the abilities by turning to true sources of healing. Temporary fixes would not resolve the problem. Harnessing the gift is not a sprint, it's a marathon.

Find Your Balance

Harnessing the empathetic gifts means finding the balance that allows you to use your abilities to help people without losing your sanity. Taking in other people's energies can knock you off balance and out of your core. Once stability is compromised, it would be difficult to stay grounded. Without balance, it is easy to become vulnerable to the influences of other people and the environment.

You cannot fully utilize your gifts and heal others if there is turmoil within yourself. Only by balancing your energy, facing your demons, and healing your wounds, can you then start to be there for the people who need your help and guidance.

Ways to harness your gift and protect yourself as an empath

1. Cut the cord

Being an empath, you radiate a positive and compassionate energy that draws people to you. Somehow, this irresistible energy gives people the license to come to you and siphon your energy for whatever purpose it serves them. As such, you unknowingly create connections and relationships that create an imbalance in your energy. It depletes you emotionally, mentally, and physically.

The problem is that even when these energy vampires have long disappeared from your life, they continue to drain you of your energy. You cannot allow this to happen, so you need to release them. The way to do this is to make a mental catalog of the people that have come in and out of your life. Decide which ones needed to go permanently and release them. This deliberate process of elimination allows you to boost your energy levels, so you have enough to focus on more meaningful pursuits.

2. Create your own sacred space

A sacred space is any place you designate as your safe spot to recharge your energy and rejuvenate your spirit. It's a place that is exclusively yours where you can pray, meditate, do yoga exercises, or write journal entries. It's a go-to-place to decompress the mind and allow the body to recuperate. The build-up of positive energy triggers the feeling of tranquility and calm that erases the distractions and mutes the noises. It's probably the only place where you can have the opportunity to connect with your higher self, allowing yourself to be comfortable with being the real you. Make it a habit of spending at least thirty minutes of your time each day in your sacred place to allow yourself to breathe.

3. Re-center your energy field

Picking up on the feelings of other people is something that's inevitable to an empath. Even if you can separate your emotions from that of others, negative thoughts and feelings can strongly influence your mindset. If you are constantly exposed to repetitive negative thoughts, the tendency is to naturally alight to negative vibrations. This then leads to blockages in the energy flow.

This becomes a problem when negative thoughts are invasive. They can accumulate over time that it becomes too difficult to shake off. This build-up must be stopped before they develop into a pattern. Re-centering your energy field is necessary so that you do not absorb the negative thoughts and emotions into your body.

One way to re-center your energy field and cleanse your aura is to meditate. Meditation balances the chakras, which are energy centers that manage and distribute the energy flow in the body. Kundalini meditation, in particular, rewires and calms the mind. By meditating, you are re-aligning yourself to your very essence which stabilizes your energy.

Another technique is mindfulness meditation. It is a method that improves focus and attention on your emotions, thoughts, sensations, and experiences in the present moment. It makes you more self-aware of your experience at the precise time you are experiencing it. Since you are only focused on the present, mindfulness meditation helps you to block out the negative noise and sensations, which enables you to calm down and maintain equilibrium.

4. Spend time in nature

Human civilization has progressed by leaps and bounds that it separates humans from what is natural. The noise and the distractions of the modern world are causing you to be out of sync with your mental and emotional energies. They can cause negative thoughts and energies to build up, which can inhibit your ability to process the emotions that you absorb from those you interact with.

Spending time in nature is not only therapeutic, but it is also purifying. By regularly taking a few hours out from your daily routine to go on a beach, a river, a park, or forest, you are reconnecting with nature and making yourself more grounded. It is a restorative experience that lets you release all the negative energies. Nature, after all, is the greatest healer.

It is necessary to understand that empaths with different types of gifts will require different needs. Not all empaths are the same. They not only have different levels of sensitivities, but they also have specializations. One training that works for one empath may not work for others. The techniques must then be tailored to match the needs of the empaths.

Chapter 7
Is Being an Empath a Superpower or a Super-Stressor?

Having the capacity to feel what others feel is something that may be perceived as a superpower. It is no different from superhumans who have psychic powers that enable them to read minds and absorb energies of people around them. Although it may sound like being a superhero character in a comic book, having empathetic abilities is really special and perhaps the closest thing to a superpower a human being could possess. But unlike in comic books, the empathetic ability is a real power that can be harnessed and put into good use.

When such ability is honed and developed properly, it can be used as a powerful tool to connect with people who need comfort, support, encouragement, or healing. Empaths who fully understand their situation tend to fully embrace their special ability, and use it to improve their psychic awareness, increase their creative output, form deeper connections with people, mend their relationships, or send healing to those who need it.

Empaths can promote change, and in that aspect, being an empath is a superpower. It must be emphasized here that empaths can have different ways to manifest their gift of empathetic ability. The experiences, manifestations, or sensations vary among empaths. With their keen sensitivities, empaths can experience the manifestation of their ability in any of the following ways: telepathy, psychometry, mediumship, physical healing, emotional healing, animal communication, nature communication, claircognizance, and geomancy.

These gifts can only be used effectively if empaths embrace what they are, and recognize that they have the power to effect change in other people's lives. If they are willing to undergo training to harness and hone their special abilities, they can take full control over their gifts. When they can manage their empathetic ability, they can use it to connect with other people and create a positive change.

On the flip side, being an empath can be a super stressor, especially to those who are untrained in the ways of empathetic ability. Empaths who lack the understanding of their gifts will find themselves caught in an emotional turmoil when they absorb other people's negative emotions. Without proper training and guidance, the heightened sensitivity can trigger a whole gamut of stressors that empaths never knew existed.

The constant bombardment of other people's energies and negative emotions is something that untrained empaths have no control of. With their heightened sensitivities, they would immediately feel the weight of the unseen stressors to the point of feeling the physical symptoms of discomfort and anxiety. This is why many empaths ended up exhausted, fatigued and weakened after prolonged exposure to all different emotions.

Not all empaths have the capability to control and harness their abilities. This is why some of them develop negative mindsets and disorders. It is extremely difficult for them to block out all the noise, which in turn, brings out a host of issues including depression, aggression, mental fatigue, bipolar disorder, and schizophrenia, to name just a few.

When empaths fail to make sense of their powerful gift, it can inadvertently affect not just their moods and emotions, but also their overall well-being. The problem is not that they are weak-willed or incapable of redirecting their sensitivities, but because the prevalence of violence, cruelty, and obscenity in this world have an undeniable effect and influence on the psyche of people who are more in-tuned to the flow of the world.

Although empaths can develop and build up their tolerance to negative energies, they will eventually have to deal with the ignored or repressed negativities that have accumulated throughout their lives. There will always be issues to deal with it, and they can be suffocating.

Whether being an empath is a superpower or a super stressor would depend on how the empath chooses to handle the gift. It can be a superpower if empaths acknowledge their abilities and put the time and effort to harness them. On the other hand, it can be a super stressor if empaths fail to recognize their abilities and fail to work on them.

Chapter 8
The Benefits of Being an Empath

Ability to impart healing energy to others

Empaths are believed to be natural healers. Since they can absorb energies from other people or objects, they can influence the flow of energy by implementing physical and mental intention and keen awareness. Through physical touch and meditation, empaths can use their energy to provide healing to people who need it. Energy healing cultivates the life force to bring back balance in all aspects of life.

Heightened senses lead to unforgettable experiences

Empaths are much more sensitive than other people. With their heightened senses, they can feel more, taste more, see more, hear more, and smell more. Experiencing things are much more enjoyable because there is always something extra to appreciate. The intensity of the experience with food, nature, sounds, views, and interaction is much more profound and makes things feel more alive.

Ability to sense danger

Empaths absorb emotions and energies and can interpret them accurately. They are more in tune with their sixth sense, so they tend to detect signs or signals that other people normally miss. They sense if something is amiss or something is out of order, it can be from a person's body language or the overall feel of a place or an environment. They can pick up ominous cues which they can use to warn people of potential risk or danger. Earth sensitive empaths can sense earthquakes, volcanic eruptions, weather disturbances, or disasters before they happen.

Keen sense of self-awareness

Having a lot of alone time adds more opportunity to be introspective and be more self-aware. Empaths have a better understanding of themselves which empowers them to make improvements in their lives and enhance their skills and abilities, especially when they interact with other people. They can recognize their uniqueness and their individuality. Hence, they can draw a line to separate their emotions from that of others. Their self-awareness also allows them to choose the people they want to surround themselves with. This is because they are acutely cognizant of what they need to become better versions of themselves.

Ability to tell if someone is sick

Empaths can tell with accuracy if a person is sick or about to get sick because they take on the feelings associated with illness and malady. Since they know if someone is not feeling well or in deep physical pain, they can provide comfort and healing when they are needed the most. Empaths can also tell if they are about to get sick. The benefit of knowing beforehand is that they can prepare and take precautionary measures to prevent the illness from manifesting.

Deeper lows, greater highs

Heightened sensitivities make empaths susceptible to experiencing deeper lows, which can have a negative impact in one's emotional well-being. However, this also means that empaths can experience greater highs, which could bring immense joy and happiness in life. All the good feelings are magnified, which can potentially drown out the negative feelings. As such, there is great enthusiasm to live life to the fullest by being more understanding, more compassionate, and more caring.

Comfortable with being alone

While many people have a fear of being alone, empaths crave for their "alone time." It is their opportunity to de-stress and shake off the negative energies that they have accumulated by interacting with people. It is also the time to recharge so that they'll have enough ammunition to endure the next days. It is in moments like this where empaths become more aware of themselves and are focused on their well-being—something they need to remain emotionally, physically, and mentally healthy.

High level of creativity

Empaths have rich experiences because of their interactions with other people. They express their encounters, feelings, and emotions through art and other outlets. Their ability to realize abstract terms and conceptualize things that are difficult to comprehend stem from their creative thought process. The more they harness their empathetic abilities, the more they can unleash their creativity. It is a way to channel all the absorbed energies.

Can read emotional cues and interpret them accurately

Empaths are very much self-aware of their sensitivities. They know that they are emotional beings, so it is easy for them to understand what other people are going through. They can sense nonverbal cues that signify what needs to be addressed. If a person is in distress, an empath can intuit what that person is going through, and what needs to be done to ease the suffering.

Ability to sense what people and creatures need

Empaths have the natural talent to sense the needs of people and creatures even if they are not spoken. They look for indicators in body language and facial expressions. Some empaths are particularly in tune with animals, plants, and the environment, so they don't have to hear spoken words to know what the creatures need or what mother nature is conveying. Empaths pick up even the slightest change in energy flow and the most subtle shift in mood and vibe.

Ability to detect lies

One of the most powerful abilities that empaths possess is the ability to detect lies. Lies can destroy relationships because they are intentional. Even though people try so hard to hide the truth deliberately, empaths can see right through the lies. Empaths can use this ability to know if someone is hiding their true feelings or covering up an objectionable act. This ability is a way to protect one's self from people with questionable intentions and those whose purpose is to take advantage of the empath's good nature.

Ability to see through the façade people put up

Apart from sensing lies, empaths can also see through the façade that many people put up to hide their feelings or their situation. People are not always ready to show their true selves until they are certain that people they interact with can be trusted. Others simply put up a wall because they fear that their real selves might be judged or rejected.

With heightened awareness and sensitivities, empaths can see right through the pretenses, and they know how to break the barriers to get through to people. This helps tremendously when empaths deal with victims who have completely shut down to help them open up their hearts and accept help.

***

There are tremendous benefits of being an empath. However, it needs to be emphasized that these benefits and advantages only manifest themselves when empaths have trained to reach their highest potential. They can only enjoy the experiences, and the special abilities if they have fully harnessed their empathetic gifts.

Having the powerful gift of empathy can be overwhelming. Managing the extraordinary gifts is necessary to reap the rewards. Empaths who are incapable of controlling and harnessing their abilities will bear the brunt of the negative effects that come with being highly sensitive. Without full control of the gifts, empaths can find themselves dealing with a host of issues including depression, fatigue, aggression, bipolar disorder, and other conditions that aggravates the negative mindsets.

It is also important to understand that empaths cannot completely block out all the noise and the energies. So, there will always be situations wherein negative mental and emotional experiences would find a way to creep in and cause a disturbance, and inadvertently affect how empaths process all the messages. It would then be difficult for empaths to separate other people's emotions from their own.

Managing, controlling, and harnessing the abilities is a life-long journey for empaths. It needs to be continuously and consistently practiced for the benefits to manifest themselves. The gift of empathy is a raw power that needs to be harnessed before the desired changes and outcomes can manifest.

Chapter 9
Ancient Knowledge and Infinite Intelligence

Human beings are intrinsically curious about objects, events, and other living creatures around them. The desire to learn leads them to investigate and delve into the unknown to the point of determining the purpose of their existence in the world. The inquisitiveness does not stop until questions have been satisfactorily answered. When answers are not convincing enough, they speculate on the possible answers and continue to challenge existing suppositions, theories, and ideas.

Questions about the nature of man and his relationship to his environment and the universe fulfill one of man's purposes—to evolve. The quest for knowledge and wisdom compels man to use his creativity to survive, thrive, and evolve. This makes him capable of possessing infinite intelligence as he fully evolves.

Infinite intelligence is often referred to as the purest energy that exists in the universe. It is contained within a single esoteric entity so powerful that it can potentially influence man's destiny in achieving his full potential. This entity is in sync and in total communication with all aspects of itself. It holds the knowledge of the entire universe—from the incalculable power of the stars above to the tiniest life form on earth. It may sound like it is an inaccessible power that only a supreme being could possess, but humans can have access to such knowledge through an ethereal link through the mind.

Throughout history, successful men and women have tapped into the power of infinite intelligence which brought them incredible knowledge, which they used to create art, invent technology, build business empires, gain tremendous wealth, and enrich their lives, and the people they had touched through their gifts. One only has to look back at the achievements of Rockefeller, Edison, Shakespeare, Da Vinci, Carnegie, Dickens, and other famous people who left an indelible mark in history.

It is believed that infinite intelligence is similar to ancient knowledge which seemed to have been lost or deliberately hidden to keep humans from acquiring them. The truth is, nothing is entirely hidden to someone who is constantly looking for answers and exploring the world beyond the physical existence. Ancient knowledge had long held the secret to unlocking man's true potential, and it's only now that humanity is taking an evolutionary leap.

With the understanding that humans are part of the eternal of the universe, man's perspective of physical existence will not be limited by physical boundaries. Man will find himself as a small segment of the infinite while being a finite being. This realization creates the awareness that the ultimate reality originates in the cosmic world and manifests in the physical world.

The wider grasp and perception of existence allows humans to evolve in such a way that the transformation allows the ideal to control the actual. It's an amalgamation of two worlds that had always been perceived as separate. This way, humans can aspire for better things beyond their perceived limits.

Infinite intelligence leads humans to the portal of mysticism to comprehend the true reality through gaining knowledge of the highest concepts of metaphysics. This then motivates human beings to transform their lives, and elevate their existence from being physical being to powerful cosmic entities capable of reaching their highest potential.

Acquiring knowledge is not just taking in a massive amount of meaningless information, it is a form of experience that connects the self with something that is more profound. Knowledge not only links the past to the present, but it also fills in the gaps. It is a medium that makes humans understand the unseen and the unknown.

People who incline to inquire and learn to gain knowledge open themselves up to infinite knowledge. Unfortunately, very few people consciously work to acquire knowledge. People, in general, merely assimilate certain phases of the full experience. They choose not to go beyond the basic knowledge of the subject matter they are learning. This is a wasted opportunity because humans are dependent on knowledge to grow, progress, and transform.

True knowledge—as opposed to an opinion or a belief—is always reliable. The knowledge process is pivotal in the transformation of man, but if no man is compelled to find the path to true knowledge, then he is bound to remain in his current state of existence. If man's perception of the metaphysical is limited to a materialistic point of view, then his final reality constitutes and values physical objects. His world would be limited in that nothing else has value beyond the material things.

Infinite intelligence is available to those who are more concerned about the absolute existence of abstract concepts rather than physical objects. If knowledge about concepts of virtue, beauty, truth, and justice is pursued, then man stands to create a life with fuller meaning and closer to the ideal life that everyone seeks. It is only elusive to those who don't realize that the inner self and the external world conspire to bring richer experiences and fuller life.

The same philosophy applies to empaths in harnessing their abilities. A limited perception of how the universe works in conjunction to how their gifts manifest would hamper their full transformation from highly-sensitive people to healers and mediums for change. It is through a clear understanding if infinite intelligence can empaths fulfill their life's true purpose.

People can only begin to grasp the power of ancient knowledge, metaphysical concepts, and infinite intelligence if there is a change in their mindset. Tapping into infinite intelligence can help unlock a wide range of opportunities that could accelerate personal growth and development.

As an empath, you can begin to understand your true self and realize that there is so much more the universe has in store for you. Infinite intelligence can help you understand your abilities and make you realize what you could become if you tap into this source of power. The force that is driving you through struggles and triumphs will shape your life experiences. Once you understand your purpose, you can make sense of the energies you absorb from other people.

Chapter 10
Why You Must Be Careful

Empathy is a good thing to have because it makes people with high sensitivities connects deeply with other people. They can sense if there is something wrong with the people they interact with. Empaths who are cognizant of their powerful gift and know how to put it into good use can help clear emotional blocks and improve the overall well-being of those they have touched. They become physical and emotional healers. In that sense, empaths bring incalculable benefits to social interaction. They are needed in an increasingly troubled society.

Although it is acknowledged widely that empaths are compassionate souls who have to fulfill a great purpose here on earth, they are not without their demons; they are, after all, humans. Not everyone talks about it, but there is a dark side to being an empath. There is a mistaken belief that all empaths are well-versed in emotions and energies that they can handle everything that they absorb. The truth is that they are more vulnerable to the harmful effects of having the powerful gift of empathy.

Empaths cannot handle their own emotions

With acute sensitivities and extreme compassion, empaths feel other people's emotions as if they were their own. When they absorb feelings of sadness, pain, or grief, they are instantly bombarded with negative energy and can sometimes crash and burn. Many of them could not distinguish between their own emotions and other people's emotions. It is always a struggle for them to make sense of what they're feeling.

They are always battling with their own emotions and sometimes they don't win and fall into depression and deep despair. Those who cannot handle the overwhelming barrage of negative emotions could end up spiraling out of control and turn to drugs and alcohol to numb their senses. They need other empaths to bring back the balance in their lives. If they don't keep their emotions in check, they are likely to develop emotional issues that could manifest physically in the form of illnesses.

Empaths are susceptible to extreme fatigue and low energy

Dealing with negative energy on a daily basis can take its toll on the body. The keen sensitivity to negative emotions and energies is not only emotionally and mentally draining, but it is also physically exhausting. Empaths deal with information overload, voluntarily or involuntarily. This means that even if they don't want to absorb the energies of other people, they have no choice because it is something that happens automatically. It does not have a switch that can be turned off when they don't feel like dealing with a range of emotions coming from strangers.

Since they are always dealing with and handling all sorts of emotions, they can quickly get fatigued. Their energies are usually low, and they feel like energy and vitality have been zapped from them.

Empaths are likely to be taken advantage of

Because of their compassion to other people, empaths always seem to believe that there is goodness in everyone. Because they are trusting souls, they sometimes cannot see that some people can be selfish and dishonest. Those kinds of people will always find a way to take advantage of others; more so of empaths who are typically kind and generous.

Empaths are targets of people who would do anything to enrich themselves by hook or by crook. Although empaths are givers by nature, they don't appreciate being taken advantage of. When they do figure out that a friend, a family member, or an acquaintance has conned them, empaths can get deeply upset that could cause them to fall into a deep depression.

Empaths tend to neglect their own welfare

Because empaths are too caught up with helping others through their gifts, they get stressed out and forget to take care of themselves. They give more importance to the welfare of others that their welfare takes a backseat. It is easy to fall into this trap not because they want to be in this situation, but because they would rather use their energies to be of service to others rather than look after their health.

If empaths continue to neglect themselves for a prolonged period, their mental and physical health can suffer. They could fall into depression due to the negative energies that they are exposed continuously too. Their low energies can make them physically weak that illnesses could start to manifest. Having the gift of empathy can be taxing to the body, so if empaths don't take care of themselves, the dire consequences could be quick.

Empaths find it extremely difficult to fall in love

Empaths find it extremely difficult to fall in love

Because empaths are exposed constantly to negative things through other people's experiences, they don't easily give themselves completely to someone. They tend to hold themselves back when it comes to falling in love because they have this nagging fear at the back of their minds that they could get hurt. With their heightened sensitivities, they are also fearful that they could not handle the extreme feeling of love and passion. This is why they keep romantic love at arm's length.

Empaths often feel they carry the weight of the world on their shoulder

Because of their selflessness and genuine concern for the welfare of other people, they feel that their role in this world is to help those who are in need. They feel that they have a responsibility to save everyone in need. While this is a noble undertaking, it places an enormous burden on them. Being who they are, they would rather carry the heavy load than to disappoint the people who rely on them for help.

As long as empaths think that they are obligated to lend a helping hand, they would continue to feel the weight of their special gift. They don't realize that the problems of the world are not their responsibility to solve.

Empaths always have to deal with conflicting voices in their heads. They feel the positive and negative energies whenever they interact with other people. Often, the intensity of energies is magnified because of their extreme sensitivities. They have developed an understanding of the world through other people's experiences, good or bad. They feel that they have a duty to save everyone from all the ugliness in the world. They feel that they could be the savior that the world needs.

What they fail to realize is that they can only do so much. They should learn to appreciate that their contribution to society is enough and it would be impossible to solve everyone's problem.

If empaths continue to carry the weight of the emotional baggage that people communicate with them, they will find themselves constantly exhausted, fatigued, and overwhelmed. If they don't learn to separate their emotions from those of others, they can quickly spiral out of control and get addicted to alcohol, drugs, or deviant behaviors. Having emphatic abilities carries a certain degree of responsibility, but empaths tend to carry that responsibility to the extreme, that they tend to neglect themselves. There is a dark side to being an empath, and without proper guidance, empaths could easily lose their way.

Although empaths are born with an extraordinary gift, they must understand that it is a raw power that must be harnessed to be used to its full potential. It is a skill that can be improved and strengthened through constant and consistent practice. Empaths have a unique role to play in this world, but they need to take care of themselves physically, mentally, and emotionally so that they can be effective healers, mediators, and catalysts for change.

CPSIA information can be obtained
at www.ICGtesting.com
Printed in the USA
LVHW052055310722
724832LV00005B/488